A TILTED WORLD

A Tilted World

Poems by

Carol Gabrielson Fine

For Charlie

Carol Gabrielson Fine

August 2018

Antrim House
Simsbury, Connecticut

Library of Congress Control Number: 2015941650

ISBN: 978-1-936482-88-7

First Edition, 2015

Printed & bound by United Graphics, LLC

Book design by Rennie McQuilkin

Front cover photograph: "Atavist" (Carl Gabrielson at Mt.
Diablo State Park, California) © 1969 by Ira W. Gabrielson

Author photograph by Hollis Dorman

Antrim House
860.217.0023
AntrimHouse@comcast.net
www.AntrimHouseBooks.com
21 Goodrich Road, Simsbury, CT 06070

for
Anne Fine and Jon Liebman,
Benjamin Fine and Julie Getzels,
Alex, Eli, Alice and Adam

ACKNOWLEDGMENTS

Grateful acknowledgment to the editors of the following publications, in which some of the poems in this volume first appeared, often in earlier versions:

Charter Oak Poets I
Charter Oak Poets II
Voices (Seabury residents' publication)

I am grateful to Amy Louise Reed (Vassar Class of 1892) who came out of retirement to teach English 105 when I was a freshman at Vassar; to Edwina Trentham, who offered my first ever poetry-writing course at Wesleyan, without which I would never have lifted poetic pen; and to Charlotte Currier, poet and teacher in the Graduate Liberal Studies Program at Wesleyan.

TABLE OF CONTENTS

Time never did assuage.

Emily Dickinson

Imperfection has a certain tang.

Adrienne Rich

A TILTED WORLD

No, I Never Expected
To Write a Poem

more complex
than those messages from
the Tooth Fairy
we tucked
under the children's pillows

or the doggerel
I slaved over to celebrate
birthdays
and bits for family –

never thought to write
all that was within
to distill
what I struggled
to keep sealed
in the cauldron within.

I did not expect that
but now
I cannot imagine
existing
without life in words.

I.

Never More Than Six or Seven

years old, no matter what,
I thought
the world had tilted
that first day I wore glasses
at six
when the living room floor
slipped sideways
though the piano never
skidded out of place,
its keyboard still at the window.

I stayed tilted,
out of place
in that flat world,
slipping, sliding on cold floors
careening on my own
dizzying path through
silent hallways,
dusty parlors,
never in focus.

Eleven

Skinny arms
skinny legs
tubby middle
no-length brown hair
glasses
those sturdy Oxfords

home from school
I let myself into the cool apartment
walk through the foyer
past the living room
blinds drawn against the autumn sun
the hammered pewter-lidded Moorcroft candy dish
on the small round inlaid coffee table
the fawn Chinese rug
its corners of blue and gold flowers
where my cousin

Eleanor
huge with her first pregnancy
sits deep in a small club chair
visiting my mother

no greeting
no smile of welcome
or cousinly embrace

no motherly after-school hug
but the quiet conversation
ceases

"El"
mother says
"she's giving you
competition"

Please

We beg of you,
we have the same last name,
we are your brother's daughters.
It is terrible here.
We are frightened.
Send for us.

So that letter to my grandfather
cried out
as my father read it aloud.
So the other letters sounded
as they trickled out for a few months
of that New York winter.

I too was frightened
seeing those elaborate strokes –
sevens with lines through them –
skittering across the pages.

From the edge of the room
I watched my father's face
for a clue.
Were those two women really
our cousins?
I wondered where they would stay.
Would they have the bedroom
I shared with my older brother?
Would I sleep in the living room,
as my mother had when
newly arrived relatives stayed with

her family when she was a girl?
Would I read far into the night
by flashlight as she had done
by gas jet?
Would Grandma and Grandpa let them
have my dead Uncle Dave's little room?

Where would they put his cello?

Chamber Music

At night through the closed door,
from afar at the front of the flat
quiet music plays.

Listening,
thinking of the warm lamplight,
I long to be there
in the circle of music stands
beside the piano.

Music stops for laughter.
Phrases are repeated.
The pianist counts out loud, sings along
to keep the tempo.
I imagine my brother turning pages as I
drift to sleep down the hall.

From the pictures my father has printed
I feel the warmth and
taste the elegant supper on the best china,
gaze on the smiling face of my mother –
animated, sparkling.

By the time morning comes
the living room is its usual
sober, somber self –
not a plate left, not a table out of place,
not a crumb on the rug,
as if I had imagined the music
in a half-dream –
a quintet playing Haydn, Dvořák, Schumann.

Still Life

Against linen folds
the regal Moorcroft vase stands tall,
round-bowled, long slender throat
glazed with summer fruit.

The nested Russian egg opened
to reveal the next lacquered layer,
a child's toy from the past, complete
until a small descendant
peeled the layers, unwittingly
let half of the tiniest center disappear
under the molding of
another dining room floor.

Mother's Staffordshire box
topped with a nosegay of china flowers,
Arnold Bennett's *Journal* worn
from years of standing
unread,
moved from house to house
with other volumes long lost.

Winey plums, rosy peaches
against navy glaze,
shiny emerald enameled egg,
pale pink, blue, creamy flowers,
worn dull green book against
pearl gray linen folds.

Life remembered in still life.

Oranges

The dingy elevator at 99 Pratt filled
with the tang of oranges
brings me back as surely as a madeleine
to summers at camp in New Hampshire,

painting the stone church in Elkins
where the tourist cabin sign next door
advertised "No Jews,"
where we all breathed
"rabbit, rabbit, rabbit…"
as we dashed past the town cemetery,

and lunchtime in the hot sun
peeling oranges,
stripping the membranes
from the sweet sections,
licking fingers
sticky with juice.

II.

Cooking Borscht

Nanny and I are making borscht
although she is not here,
has never been to Hartford.

"The burikes, Cherilah,
scrub them clean, boil them,
decant the liquid, peel them, grate them."
I see her blowing on the clear, hot, ruby liquor,
see the small ripples in the spoon's bowl.
I taste it for myself, as I did for her,
know without a doubt
that it needs more lemon,
a pinch more sugar,
another bit of salt.
Beat the eggs to a froth.
Slowly drip a spoonful at a time,
stirring rapidly.
The foamy eggs become a vivid pink.

All those childhood years
the official taster, and now
Nanny is talking me through her recipe.
Only the memory of the winey taste remains,
the rich magenta lightening to a
bright borscht hue
and finally
the quart mason jars cooling
in cold water.

Nanny is silent now, smiling.
Jars of summer borscht cool in the sink.

Everyone Knitted Argyle Socks

bobbins bouncing along the rows,
their plaiding colors crisscrossed
as the knitters played bridge or
listened to required Hygiene 105
lectures in Avery Hall.

Engaged, in time, I knitted too.
This is how it was – you
became engaged,
knitted socks for your man.

"Let's give them to Dad."
"But I made them for you."
"But Dad will love them."

I never knew if he wore them but I
was never asked for another pair
until much later
I made them bootie-size
for Ben,
multicolored feet kicking
above the carriage rim.

Processional

Self-conscious
on display
like the groom on the wedding cake
absently gazing straight ahead
arms hanging straight at his sides
silently
walking next to his daughter
across the living room
past the string quartet playing
softly near the piano
out through the porch

down the aisle
slowly
her kid-gloved hand sliding
against his arm

he offers no compliment
no "left right"
to be sure they start together
no last fond word as
he walks her through the congregation

If he smiles
she does not see
veiled glance blurred without glasses

In front of the flowered chuppah
he steps aside
without a goodbye kiss
without a goodbye pat

Her kid-gloved hand slides to her side

Missing the Bus

Through grimy bus windows on Fifth Avenue
I see the sign at 46th Street,
the scurrying figure,
a dark-haired man, flushed, gray-suited,
carrying a brief case.

Startled at the hissing of the
doors, the broken-field running of the man,
I recognize my father, tearing for the bus
as it pulls away from the curb
without him.

Retired because of a heart attack,
silenced by his own mortality,
idled against his will, still running,
still impatient, frantic with free time,
my father is seized
with activity – flute lessons,
Chinese brush painting, yet another camera.

I cannot bear to watch as the bus
lurches into traffic,
wonder which train he is rushing to catch,
imagine how furious
he'll be
at the gate
slammed shut.

Father

My brother and I never called him anything but
Father. My daddied friends thought it weird,
laughed uncomfortably.

I never called him Dad –
we didn't.
He was always Father.

Even today
my brother and I refer to him
as Father.

On the way to his burial thirty-three years ago,
I heard my brother say he always knew
Father loved him.

I had no word to add,
did not know,
did not assume.

Seeing My Father

On Main and Asylum shoppers dash
like ants scurrying from stepped-on anthills.
Near the corner without thinking
I begin to run,
almost calling after
a fading figure –
the impatient walk,
the square shoulders on the tense body.

People bump into me, glaring
lunchtime shoppers,
prisoners of the clock,
as he begins to fade into the crowd.

But I keep running
as if I could touch him,
as if I could throw myself into his arms,
as if he would notice.

People of Memory

Late afternoon sun through stained glass
dappled white gloves into
shards of ruby and sapphire as
we sat all afternoon at the side aisle,
stood for Kaddish,
remembered, prayed for father,
for grandparents,
for we are a people of memory –

just the two of us as the afternoon lengthened,
those jeweled blurs fading,
the joyous notes of Neilah, and the shofar
sounding as we knew it would,
as it has always sounded.

All that long afternoon with the sun
streaming over us as the day closed, we sat,
just the two of us,
putting aside our different natures:
mother and daughter
remembering the past,
finding comfort in just being together,
in knowing
that we are a people of memory.

III.

Consciousness Raising

passed me by
though I'd heard of Betty Friedan,
Gloria Steinem, Simone de Beauvoir.

Where was I
that I did not know
it was for me too –
daughter, wife, mother,
daughter-in-law, sister, aunt,
breadwinner, laundress, cook,
chauffeur, PTA president, shop steward…

My life was fine:
I had a husband,
children,
work that helped others,
my own bank account –
liberated
to work full time plus
the swing shift till midnight,

devoted to my husband and
my children,
my mother,
my brother.

How can I say it would have helped
when I was lost
long before
in the chill
of my childhood?

Anxiety

and I are a pair
inseparable as meiotic cells,
divide yet cleave.
We go everywhere together,

inseparable as schoolgirls
wearing the same colors,
liking the same records,
never making a move
without the other.

Anxiety guards me jealously,
fearing I may slip away,
making sure I never leave,
never know more
than fleeting peace.

Sansevieria

plant also known as Mother-in-law's Tongue

I fix dinner in the cramped yellow kitchen
after all day at the cash register
after all week in five schools.
My mother-in-law stalks me,
following from place to place:
the sink to wash lettuce,
the stove to stir horseradish sauce,
the table to set,
the tongue to slice.

She watches me,
waiting to pounce
while the men rest in the living room,
does not offer help.

The sauce is too thick,
I should never have tried a new recipe.

She sticks to my side
as I carry plates to the table.
Luckily I do not drop one.
Back and forth we go
like two ocelots indoors at the zoo.

Dinner nearly ready,
she leaps –
her last chance as I slice the tongue:

"How come you haven't had a child?
There's–well–his daughter–ah–you know…"

Yes, I know.
Yes, it is nearly four years.

She doesn't know the endless tests,
the humiliating questions,
charts,
biopsies,
the scheduled couplings.

She doesn't know.
Good wife that I think I am,
I do not tell her.

Late First Stage

Why am I here?
I don't want to be here.
They said it wouldn't hurt
if you breathed right.

I don't want to take care of anyone.
I'm all alone.
It's three in the morning.
My husband's gone home to sleep.
How can he sleep?

In his starched shirt and tie
my doctor's up on the hospital roof
watching for Sputnik.
In a dim corner of the Labor Room
out of sight
a nurse knits.

I don't want to be a mother.
I'm forgetting to breathe,
to rest in between.
I'm scared.

"Pregnancy is only a condition,"
my father used to say,
"not a disease."

Why do I feel so alone?
Get him off the roof!
Tell him I've decided
it's not the right time.
I don't want to be anybody's parent.

Postpartum Joy

"One more push," my doctor said –
"It's a girl!"
Of course. I had a daughter
just as I had hoped.

My landladies marveled
at how tiny she seemed,
"like a $1.98 doll," they said.

Learning to talk, she watched me,
moving her lips as I spoke.
"I do it myself."

As I left for work
a few months before her brother was born,
she ran, plucked knitted hat, gloves and scarf
from the bottom bureau drawer,
gleefully put them on, and danced about,
crowing.

The morning after I brought Ben home
from the hospital, she climbed on his crib
and announced, "OK, baby stay."

Last Rites

At the first of many farewells
we stood,
Anne, Benjamin, and I,
under the apple tree
in a late afternoon summer drizzle.

We'd found Blue Boy, Anne's parakeet,
possibly poisoned by paint fumes,
motionless on his back
on the floor of his cage.
Such a tiny bird to feel so heavy.

A slipper box seemed the right size
for a coffin.
So many tears
as we laid him in the padded box,
the empty cage so pitiful.

The children chose a spot under
the apple tree, dug a small hole,
covered him with earth,
marked the spot with summer flowers.

We sang Taps.
Rain dripped through apples and leaves
onto their yellow slickers and red boots.

Side by Side

They sit on the altar
in highbacked velvet armchairs,
my small son and his father.

Standing on a wooden box
so he can be seen
over the pulpit desk,
the only grandson in his father's family
leads the congregation,
chants blessings before and after his
Torah and Haftorah portions.
Seriously and tunefully he
reads and sings.

At the last exultant note
of the concluding blessing
for the privilege of reading,
he breathes out quietly,

steps down,
walks with dignity
back to the armchair
next to his father
who smiles proudly but
does not embrace him.

As he sits down
he takes his borrowed handkerchief
from the breast pocket of his new navy blazer,
wipes his small face,

unfogs his glasses
just as the rabbi might
at the end of a sermon
on such a humid day.

Grandfather is called
to the Ark,
his honor to replace
cover and ornaments of the Torah.
He dresses it
as he has dressed his
store window models,
tense,
expressionless.

They stand then, the three of them,
my husband now
at his father's side.

I am faced with the striking
resemblance admitted only now.
I am afraid.

Looking for Hermann Broch's Grave

The gates on Grove Street were locked,
the iron pickets spiked high above her head,
sharp, menacing, but her husband
was determined to get her over the top.

She turned away, but he seized the moment,
making it his adventure,
snagging his slacks as he swung over
to trespass in a graveyard,
not caring why they hunted
for someone he'd never heard of.

He thrust his hand through the bars
to make a step, grabbed her hand,
ordered her to jump
from the top of those rusted spears to
the moldy ground,
the same way he'd once made her
sit in front
as they rode a sled
careening
down Lookout Hill in Keney Park.
He'd crowed with glee.
She'd cried then, too.

She dropped
as if he had pushed her.

Without a map, without a guide,
they trudged those rows,

his triumph forgotten
as quickly as the moment,
faster even than the chill
of autumn twilight,
a dying marriage,
his slashed trousers a mourner's badge.

Strangers

We didn't know
you didn't know me
and I
stranger to myself
did not know
did not want to know
me

Too busy doing
to be
too busy
trying to keep from knowing
we did not know ourselves
did not know each other
could not know each other
did not want each other to know

afraid
we might not like
what we might
find

Ten Years It Is

from that day you closed the door
at five on a January morning
leaving the bleakness of our life
for another world
I could not share.

When you died after five years away
you weren't mine to lose
yet I lived again those first days,
knew again the pain
of new grief,
of new-found freedom,
of being alone in
a Noah's Ark world.

We never made it to the golden years,
those years when couples
become couples again
when they reclaim each other
or
lose each other
all over again.

No Place

Society has no place for me.
He isn't mine to grieve.

In different ways
my children grieve.
I too know what it is to lose a father
before he ever had a chance
to know me grown up,
before he had a chance
to be my children's grandfather.

He isn't mine to grieve.
I have already mourned
for his leaving,
still mourn alone
for what never was.

I mourn the aloneness
greater even than marriage's,
the absence of shared memories,
of hoped-for sharing
even when we were together.

Kaddish isn't recited
for a marriage
or an ex-husband.

One remembers only
for oneself –
for the life no longer,
for the love no longer.

IV.

Harvest

I remember the first time we grew them –
in a victory garden,
a small plot once full of flowers
now turned to the war effort.
Big Boys we grew.
City-bred, waiting for that perfect moment,
my father and grandmother dashed out,
salt shaker in hand, vying to be first.
They ate them like apples.
Lush, juicy, skins firm but not
tough, like this year's.

Maybe it is the drought,
the erratic watering –
tough skins protect them from drying out.
Perhaps it is the variety – small,
not the sensuous Beefsteaks of memory.

Or is it that age has stolen my taste buds
as it has my dark hair, or
that memory deceives me
into dreaming
a lusciousness that never was?

Warm November

Oriental maples –
tiny leaves clinging
past frost
gleam like rubies
through late afternoon sun,
sparkle boldly against
the faded green house
across Cumberland Rd.

These jewels cheer me,
these crimson butterflies
that will flutter soon
to the ground
to fade,
dry to a papery crunch
before being swept
to the curb.

One I press
at the beginning
of the *M's*
in my dictionary.

Autumn Storm

Yesterday the wind screamed,
rains came after dark,
hesitant at first, then in torrents.

Cars blustered by,
muddy spray half blinding me.

Relief came as I turned into my driveway.
Random leaves plastered the macadam
into a vivid magic carpet.

This morning the sun is bright,
tapestry muted
russet, silvery brown, ochre and garnet.

The trees stand threadbare.

My Contemporary

The aged tree offers
a late life triumph.
Gnarled branches bow
with unaccustomed weight.

Apples fall day and night,
gnawed or slightly wormy,
thudding the grass.

Long ago the branches
were closer to the ground.
I could pick the fruit myself.
Applesauce, pies in a good year,
more than I wanted.

But now
the apples are out of reach,
a gift to crows and squirrels.
More fruit there is this summer
than in the past five years
together.

The grass is carpeted with apples,
yellow jackets.
A cidery smell fills the yard.

McKinnon and I and Brahms

In the high-ceilinged white living room where
the faded red butterfly chair cradles me
slinglike in its black metal frame,
I sit facing the fading afternoon,
McKinnon curled at the window,
soaking up hazy November sun.

Capriccios and intermezzi
sparkle across the room as I watch
the sky slip from rose and blue
to lavender and gray.

The long window frames
gnarled black branches of the catalpa
into a Japanese print,
broad pads of yellow leaves
flapping against skinny pods.

Listening, sketching tree and sky until
the music stops,
I feel the silence after the brilliance
of Richard Goode.
The sky has softened, grayed, as
McKinnon stirs,
stands noiselessly on the sill,
swishes her tortoise shell tail and
springs silently
to the floor.
She pads softly toward me,
rubs against the metal frame.

Sunapee Mikveh

mikveh: ritual bath

I.

I thought I had forgotten the sweet
fragrance of the lake,
the pleasure of water.
There had been nothing to keep
that memory before me.
But I had not forgotten
its soothing coolness,
the unimpeded view of the furrowed bottom,
sandy ridges that stay –
no dried skate cases,
no calico scallop shells sand-polished,
only last year's pine needles,
shreds of bark settled to the bottom,
cushioning my feet.

II.

The mountains have vanished again.
Drizzle.
The air is damp and heavy.
A rowboat moored near the point rocks,
turns gracefully,
stern out toward deeper water.
A grave wooden owl guards the dock.
Ducks wait in the reeds along the shore.
Maple and spruce branches dip

ever so slightly.
I shall not disturb the stillness
when I walk into the water,
swim a few strokes barely
breaking the surface.
I'm going nowhere in fog and water.

III.

I have had my ritual bath
even though I have not dunked three times,
no one inspected my fingernails
or watched as I walked into the lake,
no one pronounced me kosher
as I emerged,
pleasantly chilled,
my skin soft,
my soul restored.

V.

Thinking of Ben at Sunapee

I waited for you in the unexpected June heat,
ankles swollen in canvas sneakers,
ten days past your estimated time of arrival,
nineteen days past your father's guess.

Thirty-seven years later
a stalled air mass over Sunapee
makes it too hot to go outside.

Tomorrow is your birthday.
Now I wait only to exchange a few words
long distance.

Tricks of Time

One windy day blew into the next.
Icy walks led to that shabby
yellow brick school
where worn-out varnished floors creaked.

Then the revelation
that the year is a round thing, that seasons
will roll over the top into place,
that winter will follow the golden fall,
spring, summer will come again.

Now time telescopes.
Once endless days
spill
one into the other.
No longer can I say
my hair is pewter
as once I said
it was chestnut.

It is getting white,
white as clear winter days,
whiter
when summer comes again.

Lacunae

The fabric of family, friends,
community
begins to wear thin.
Once threads were closely woven,
so tightly sometimes
there seemed no room to move.
Little by little the strands
sag, letting in light
though the filaments remain
able to catch us in a net.

Then without our consent
the yarn frays, the weave
becomes threadbare
like heels of socks –
holes so large
the webs that supported us,
patterned our lives
snap,
leaving us hanging slack,
reaching in vain for a familiar lifeline.

Sleepless

I wander about
downstairs,
head pounding, lungs gasping,
waiting for the kettle to boil.

As the sky lightens
I sit at the kitchen table,
sipping tea, daydreaming.
It is no longer night
though not yet day.

In the full-length mirror on the door,
as steam rises from the cup
I watch myself
thinking
this is how it must have been.

Grandma, what woke you –
your memories
or your empty days?
No longer needed,
you lived each day alone
in your small, dark apartment,
haggling with your tenants,
hanging your meager laundry
in the gritty airshaft.

Did you wonder about your life
as I wonder about you,
the grandmother I hardly knew,

or did you
just exist
alone,
unable to emerge
from your own darkness?

Block Island

in memory of Joan Egeland-Scott

The other day, just off the ferry to Block Island,
I looked for you as we trundled in an old, cranky
yellow school bus along narrow rutted roads
crowded with cyclists, cars, motorcycles and
helmeted school children on bicycles.
Accompanied by the driver's gossip about
"natives," we bounced past weathered cottages and
your endless stone walls.
Some were hidden, overgrown by rugosa roses,
rich with their smooth, ripe orange hips.
Some meandered across the furze-covered
dark green hills.

So many little white picket fences.
So many different kinds of glacial stones.
Which cottage was yours?
Which wall holds your moonstone quartz?

I saw you as a little girl dancing
into the surf, splashing back as a bigger wave
menaced you.
I saw you gathering driftwood on the town beach,
picking wild blueberries and fox grapes,
dropping clusters into your tin pail.

I know you through memories of childhood,
through poems about Howie, your teenage son,
about his last swim in the cold Maine river.

You seemed hopeful the last time
we met for poetry at your Young Street flat.
We didn't know you had so little time.

I wanted to see you on your island,
to hear you read poems again,
to have you show me your home,
tell me about all those stone walls.

Yom HaShoah

In the darkened sanctuary,
the setting sun illuminating
stained glass windows
with only the reading lamp and
the Eternal Light above
shining on the lectern,
we read all day
name after name
from morning to
the beginning of Shabbat services:
first name – last name –
father's name – age – place of residence –
place of death – year of death.
Whole families, from grandfathers,
grandmothers to tiny children,
sometimes a familiar name,
perhaps a lost relative,
perhaps not, but
strangers no more.

After the last name on my page
I stand silent, trembling, then
walk slowly across the altar
to take the Torah scroll from
the one who read before me,
to sit as witness in a high
wooden pulpit chair until
I think I cannot bear to hear
another name, cannot stop shaking but,
as I in turn pass the Torah to next reader,

the names continue.

Four thousand names we read,
four thousand of the six million.
It takes eight hours.
Strangers no more.

Nobody

calls late at night anymore –
really late, near midnight,
telling of wonderful chamber music concerts
heard spur of the moment at Tully Hall,
the sheer triumph of buying the last single ticket,
hearing a quartet play Brahms, live,
then finding a taxi for the long ride downtown
with always that touch of apprehension,
the knowledge that late night jaunts are not safe
for old ladies.

Sometimes late at night, I imagine
the phone ringing, imagine her telling me
where she's been, what she's done,
telling me she wishes we'd had more
than these small moments.

Is There WiFi in the Afterlife?

in memory of Ira Wilson Gabrielson

Wherever you are, I bet *The New York Times*
has a delivery route.
Have you subscribed? Or no…you changed
to online; it was much less expensive.
You wouldn't even have to look for a pen.

You sometimes called me on a Saturday.
Once, by phone, we shared the crossword.
Could we share another?
It wouldn't have to be a Saturday.
Do you even have Saturdays?

Is your Mac always on? Is it wireless?
Do you chat?
Anytime after 8 a.m. would be fine.

VI.

Sorting Faded Photographs

stored in shoeboxes,
we find ourselves in others.
Great, great grandmother
sober in her black wig,
stern for the unaccustomed camera.
She attended a thousand births,
never lost a mother, they said.
Her name is on my mother's
birth certificate in New York City Hall.
How did she get to this country,
this woman I know only in pictures or
scant stories?
How did she
get a license, learn a language?

Nanny, serious in her finest dress,
poses with two of her sisters
under a backyard tree, perhaps
at their mother's in Albany,
so like Chekhov's sisters in their orchard.
We catch glimpses of ourselves
in fading portraits.

Six generations later
my daughter is the midwife.
Young, her dark hair gathered in a ponytail,
her straight-lashed eyes warm,
she shows her toddler son
pictures in an album,
not in shoeboxes,

not posed in stiff dresses or best suits
for a once-in-a-lifetime memento,

but people of the present
who sometimes look
so much like those
remembered in one solemn pose,
remembered in fragments
handed down
from one generation
to the next
to my daughter and her son.

In Light We Remember

Once again the brass menorah polished
glistens softly
as I strike the match to light
candles, one more each night,
kindled in memory of a miracle.
Only oil enough to last one night yet
it burned for eight.
The candles flicker as I sing for myself
the blessings I sang with my children.

In light we are seen, in light we remember
though we are seen no more.

Then I turn to light the single candle
in its heavy tumbler –
Yahrzeit for my father who might have shrugged
but for whom I light the glass candle
as I lit candles that last night
of Hanukkah.
He died
just as the flames guttered.

Now my daughter lights them
for her boys who
love candles,
who do not know
more than that yet –
just that they glow and flicker as
they learn the same blessings I sang
with their mother and uncle.

In light we are seen, in light we remember
though we are seen no more.

Below the Trinity Rocks

the red light changes.
Ahead, Zion Street is empty,
except for the lights of a bodega,
a few bars,
then at Bonnell
the lime-green *Sprite*
in Timothy's plate glass window.

It's past hours but one still
glimpses wooden booths,
the grill hood, the stained glass
suncatcher with its wide smile.

I think of another *Sprite*
at the corner of Wissahickon Ave.
and Naomi St.
the day after Alex was born.
A small abandoned grocery.
Above it
in a gerrymandered half-house
lived my daughter, her husband,
and now their first-born.

"My granddaughter living over a store!"
I could hear my mother's shocked voice
had she lived to greet
her first great grandchild.

I See My Daughter

mothering her baby,
laughing at him
as his drooly hands flail at her face,
whispering
"Alex, be patient,
we're just changing sides"
as he stuffs those fingers into his
mashed-banana-coated mouth,
smiling amused when his father says
"Alex, you have the table manners of a goat"
as she philosophically mops his chins.

I tell her
she never drooled,
never spit up.

"That's my boy," she glows –
exuberant Alex
crowing at each new skill,
blowing raspberries.

I must have done better than I thought
for her to give so lovingly.

Annie Alexander

I've heard about her
but have no idea
who she really was,
what she looked like,
where she fit in the family picture,
whose second cousin she may have been,
whose sister-in-law perhaps.

She was always called that
to distinguish her from Annie,
my grandmother, sometimes called
Little Annie
to distinguish her from
Big Annie, her closest friend,
who lived upstairs on Belmont Avenue.

Now there's Alexander's Annie,
Alex's mother,
my daughter
whom I never expected to be called
Annie.
It seemed dated.
The nicknames we tried never clicked
until one by one
her friends began to call her
Annie,
the name by which she signs her letters,
somehow no longer old-fashioned.

Mrs. Noah

I've asked all over but
no one knows why Mrs. Noah
is missing from the wooden ark
I bought, roughly carved,
unpainted with its small ladder,
removable blue roof.

All those pairs of animals for Alex
to march into the ark.

Alex lines up zebras, elephants,
tigers and sheep, giraffes –
all couples
as Noah waits for them.

Is Mrs. Noah dicing onions in the galley
or making up beds for her family?
Is she checking off the animals
from some master list
as they climb aboard,
lumbering, hopping or flying up the ladder,
assigning a place for each or
tapping her foot impatiently
as she waits
for Japheth,
always the last to appear
when called for dinner?

At Lulu's with Alex

Like two boulevardiers we sit in the sun,
utterly contented, he with his croissant, I
with my decaf capuccino which he drains
when it is cool.
"What if that tree had a thousand colors
in its leaves?
When will you be ninety, Granny?
Where will you be when I am ninety?"

For now, we compare
veins,
his not visible, mine all too,
read, build blocks together,
walk, even play baseball.
I smile graciously when he announces,
"Granny, I beat you by three."

The sun warms us at Lulu's
until Alex is ready to get his scooter.
"Trust me," he says,
"I know another way home."

"I'm an Artist"

Eli says. "That's what everyone says
at Leila Day."

Abstract impressionist at four –
purple, brilliant blue, green,
that splash of shocking pink
swirling off-center.

A delicate, ghostly green pirate ship
glides across the page, almost
disappears in a morning mist.

The fire engine races to its call,
firemen poised to leap.

Prehistoric horses prance
across the sky,
spindly legs on oblong bodies.

One day a silvery, sparkly oval
moon arrives in the mail.
For you, Granny.

Mother cuts a string of paper people.
Eli colors them, each a different person.
"Don't put them on the refrigerator,
Granny," he says as he colors their backs.

"I'm doing my work, Granny.
Please don't look."

Grace Notes

1.

Alice at 2 races down Greenwood,
spins onto Montrose.
Running after, I worry about traffic.
She squats on the sidewalk.
Someone has scribbled letters.
Alice points, says each
in her strong voice.
A young man stops, astonished.
"She's reading," he gasps.
"Just letters," I explain.

2.

Alice at 2 watches McKinnon the Cat strut past.
"So, McKinnon, what's the deal?"

3.

At "Winnie the Pooh" Ben lifts Alice at 3 over the first
row of seats so she can join the cast in a tug of war with
Eeyore. A tiny figure with glasses.

4.

Alice at 4 introduces yoga poses at a recital, since she is
the only one in a class of adults who can pronounce them.

5.

I'm reading to Alice. She's about 4
and doesn't usually let adults read to her.
I read "ballet."
She takes her thumb from her mouth.
"No, that's *ball-et.*"
"It's a French word," I say –
"a kind of dancing."
"Oh." The thumb is replaced.

6.

In kindergarten:
Teacher asks for words that end in an O sound.
Alice says "eau."
Teacher, puzzled, asks her to come to the chalkboard.
Alice writes "Eau."

7.

Grandma opens her Shakespeare, turns
to "To be or not to be,"
asks Alice, circa 5, if she would like to read it.
With the book propped on the bookcase,
Alice reads the soliloquy without hesitation,
as if auditioning for the part –
straight through she reads
without a mistake
or even a pause,
knows instinctively it's a poem.

8.

At Intelligentsia
while Alice is at nursery school
Ben has coffee.
Adam at 2 shares Ben's coffee cake,
walks around the tables, sings
"Be kind to your parents
though they don't deserve it."
When I visit and ask
for a repeat performance,
he smiles to himself, won't perform.

9.

Time for dessert.
Time for a game.
We try to guess something
on 2-year-old Adam's face.
Nose. No. *Eyes.* No. *Eyelashes.* No.
We go on and on.
We give up.
"Cwumbs," says Adam.

10.

I'm visiting in Chicago.
Alice is about 5.
She asks me to make French Toast
for her (late breakfast).
I'm not sure where everything is.

She tells me a few times, then says,
"I think you'd better ask Adam.
He's more into cooking than I am."
Adam at 3 is Ben's sous-chef.

11.

Ben: "How much is 15 + 15?"
Adam (4): "30"
Ben: "How did you get it?"
Adam: "10 + 10 + 5 + 5."

12.

Adam has to keep a journal in 5th Grade.
One page has *I really really really*
all down the page until
don't like writing in my journal.

13.

Adam, Ben, Anne and Jon are playing
Hearts. Adam (16 now) is also doing
his calculus homework. It's a smooth
transition from game to work,
back and forth.

14.

Snuggled into his mother's coat,
only his rainbow-striped cap
peeking out, three-month-old Eli

rides the commuter train.
No need for a dining car.
Satisfied,
he sighs.
His mittened hand rests
across his mother's coat.
"Finished your snack?" asks
a man across the aisle,
rising to debark at his stop.

15.

Eli at 2 rides in the shopping cart,
watches as each item is deposited
behind him.
Anne reads from her list.
Eli nods.
"Julie, Ben, and Baby Alice are coming…
Oh!" She turns down another aisle.
"We need diapers for Alice."
Eli, indignant:
"Alex *not* wear diapers."

16.

I've taken Alex and Eli to the Peabody
while Anne is at work.
Alex (5½) wants me to buy him
a small stuffed dog. I ask Eli (2½)
if he wants something. He moves
the tiny frogs around, notices
two together. "They're mating."

17.

Eli is 3. We're at Friendly's on Park Rd.
We're getting ready to leave,
Alex, Eli and Anne to New Haven
and I home. Eli tells Anne
they have to take me there – I'll be lonely
if I have to go by myself.

18.

Eli sends a thank-you note that has
printed on it *The part I enjoyed most
about Grandparents' Day…*
Eli's answer: *was being with you.*

ABOUT THE AUTHOR

Carol Gabrielson Fine is a graduate of Vassar College, Clark University, and Wesleyan University's Graduate Liberal Studies Program, under whose auspices she earned a second Masters degree forty years after her first. Had she believed in the advice of her freshman year English professor at Vassar, Amy Louise Reed, she might have written poetry sooner. Instead, she became a nursery school teacher, school psychologist, and research psychologist working with deaf and hard-of-hearing children. At Wesleyan she began writing poetry in the classes of Edwina Trentham and Charlotte Currier, and shortly thereafter was the invited reader in the Prosser Poetry Series at Prosser Library in Bloomfield, CT. A sometime art student, she painted in her younger days and has always been a devotee of chamber music, opera, and theater.

In addition to membership in several poetry groups, she has been a member of the Social Justice Committee of Congregation Beth Israel, coordinating work at soup kitchens and knitting hundreds of winter caps for Hartford children in the after-school program at Charter Oak Cultural Center. As a member of the West Hartford Interfaith Housing Coalition, she worked to procure affordable housing; and as a founding member of Adventures Together, she seeks to foster interfaith understanding through book discussions involving members of Congregation Beth Israel and the Bethel African Methodist Episcopal Church.

Carol Fine is the mother of two children, the grandmother of four, an aunt and great aunt many times over. She lives at Seabury in Bloomfield, Connecticut.

This book is set in Garamond Premier Pro, which had its genesis in 1988 when type-designer Robert Slimbach visited the Plantin-Moretus Museum in Antwerp, Belgium, to study its collection of Claude Garamond's metal punches and typefaces. During the mid-fifteen hundreds, Garamond—a Parisian punch-cutter—produced a refined array of book types that combined an unprecedented degree of balance and elegance, for centuries standing as the pinnacle of beauty and practicality in type-founding. Slimbach has created an entirely new interpretation based on Garamond's designs and on compatible italics cut by Robert Granjon, Garamond's contemporary.

To order additional copies of this book
or other Antrim House titles, contact the publisher at

Antrim House
21 Goodrich Rd., Simsbury, CT 06070
860.217.0023, AntrimHouse@comcast.net
or the house website (www.AntrimHouseBooks.com).

•

On the house website
in addition to information on books
you will find sample poems, upcoming events,
and a "seminar room" featuring supplemental biography,
notes, images, poems, reviews, and
writing suggestions.